SELECTED POEMS

SELECTED POEMS

DIANA DER-HOVANESSIAN

The Sheep Meadow Press
Riverdale-on-Hudson, New York

All inquiries and permission requests should be addressed to:
The Sheep Meadow Press, Post Office Box 1345,
Riverdale-on-Hudson, New York 10471.

Designed and Typeset by the Sheep Meadow Press.
Printed on acid-free paper in the United States. This book
meets the guidelines for permanence and durability of the
Committee on Production Guidelines for Book Longevity of
the Council on Library Resources.

Library of Congress Cataloging-in-Publication Data

Der-Hovanessian, Diana
        [Poems. Selections]
        Selected poems.
            p.   cm.
        ISBN 1-878818-27-9
            1. Armenian American–Poetry.   I. Title.
PS3554.E67A6   1994
811'.54–dc20   94-1260
                                                        CIP

CONTENTS

ACKNOWLEDGMENTS

Grateful acknowledgment is made to the editors of the following periodicals where many of these poems first appeared: *Agni, American Scholar, American Literary Review, Andover Review, Ararat, Boston Review, Christian Science Monitor,* (Copyright Christian Science Monitor Publishing Company), *Ezra Pound Anthology, The Forum, Graham House Review, Harper's Magazine, Literary Review, Louisiana Review, Lyric, McCall's, Nation, New Republic, New York Times, Paris Herald Tribune, Poetry Now, The Poetry Review, Raft, Sail, Sands, Stone Country, Southern Poetry Review, Worcester Review, Yankee.* Thanks are also due to Jack Antreassian, editor of Ararat Press, publisher of *How To Choose Your Past*, and Ashod Press: *Songs of Bread, Songs of Salt*, and *About Time*. Grateful acknowledgement also to Deborah Baker and Stanley Moss for selecting these poems from the above three books.

SELECTED POEMS

SALT

I

It was unnecessary long ago
to perspire. And salt
had not been discovered.
It took medieval pain
and pressure, the worry
over fate and free
will to make man sweat.

Then salt crystallized and those
who discovered it lived
in an Armenian village called Koghb.

Since that day
the Greeks in books of alchemy
labeled salt, sal armenicum
in deference to the origins of
alum, malachite and lazulite.

Along the river Vardamark,
along the Arax and Akhurian
through the valley Aghto
traders came, by oxcart
and caravan along Salt Road
to the mines
of Nakhichevan, Keghzvan
from the west
until the railroad's time.

From the east another horde
decided there might be
a better way to speed
the supply
by making the Armenians
weep and weep.

II

But do not think salt came
from Armenia only
from sadness.
Tears come from laughter too.

Salt remains when the sea recedes,
when the flood subsides.
It is what is
when passion is cased
to coat the face of calm.

The same salt that flavors
the table sweetens the breath,
causes the blood to rise, spoils
the pilaf and brightens the smile.
Salt that eats the heart
can erode the sun.

When you throw it over
your left shoulder to blind
the eye of Bad Luck
invite Good Luck to your table,
and say with the Armenian poets

"Hey, djan,
let us toast one another,
the dispersed;

"but don't let the salt
of longing close our throats
with thirst.

"Hey, djan,
our differences, like salt,
flavor what we eat.

"But let us not consume
more salt than meat."

BREAD

Something to sandwich
around building blocks
in nutrition charts.

Or leave behind
in restaurants
to be thrown out.

Who thinks of tassled
wheat, or sacred wafers?
Or thin arms stretching

toward marching armies,
waiting?
Who thinks of it at all?

TWO ARMENIANS WALKING ON SUNDAY

1.
Walking with an Armenian
is different
from walking with anyone
else.
In the first place
he will try to catch
up with another Armenian
unless you happen to be one.
In the second place
he will keep looking
sideways for another Armenian
unless you happen to be one.

Laughing with an Armenian
is different
from laughing with anyone
else.
You know
you're laughing because
you've survived.

2.
He'll lead you off the path
and like tassled whips
the grass will beat lightly
against your legs
as you plough through
for motion
not direction,
for denseness that makes a path.

3.
"What does that butterfly
mean? The one that flies
over your head"

"Is it a Monarch
or Phantom Blue?"

"It's white.
Small and white."

"That's one of the ghosts
of the 34 Armenian dialects
inquiring into
our quiet."

4.
When two Armenians
are quiet it is not
because there isn't anything to say.

THE DREAM

"Children of massacre,
children of destruction,
children of dispersion,
oh, my diaspora..."
someone was calling
in my dream.
Someone was explaining
why Armenian children
are raised with so much
wonder, as if they
might disappear
at any moment.
"Tsak. Tsakoug."
Someone was explaining
why Armenian sons love
their mothers to excess,
why daughters-in-law are
cherished, why mothers-
in-law are treasured,
why everything
is slightly different
in an Armenian home,
stared at,
as if it might melt.
Someone was telling me
why Armenians love
earth and gardening so much
and why there is a hidden rage
in that love.
Someone was explaining
why I surround
myself with green plants
that do not flourish
in spite of great care.
"The slant of the sun is wrong."
Someone was gently chiding
for the strange angle of

my outside plants.
Someone was saying
I spoke English with a slight accent
even after three generations.
Someone was calling
in a forgotten language.

DIASPORA

I am the tourist
who looks just like
the native girl
who greets me, salt
and bread on her tray.

We have the same eyes,
the same smile and stride
but different tongues
with which to say.

I am the stranger
in my father's land,
the traveler to the country
I can neither leave
nor stay,
a foreigner in the place,
where milleniums ago
my kind was bred.

I am no one
without these trees, these stones
and streets. But their shadows
have grown short and tall without my weight.

I am the tourist
from far away
where I left the tables of plenty
thirsty and unfed.

THE BAKER'S APPRENTICE

Sunday. The only day
I did not rise before the sun
to light my ovens.

But I was wakened by
the sound of feet moving
over the streets.

It was the day of the exodus
in our small city Mazera.
I was told to stay

because I was a baker,
spared the march,
told to wait until

"the others came back
when the state
was stabilized."

Families with supplies
for a day's walk shuffled
along. I wanted to go too

or give them something. Bread.
The smell of baking bread,
my daily gift. My gift

that spared me while Bedros
who made shoes was taken
although he had not been

conscripted into the army earlier.
This time his clever apprentice,
his twelve-year-old son was kept.

Next door, the priest
at the boys' school and his
charges formed a double line.

All except one who had come
the night before to
my back door for bread.

He intended to travel by dark
to his village to check
on his family. I cut a cross

into his loaf, the last
I served that way. Two years
later a Turkish apprentice

was brought into my store
by two black mustached gendarmes
who introduced him.

I had already guessed
his name.

THIS IS FOR ZARIF

who used to draw
in the mud of the water bank
with a stick and weave marvelous
stories for her little boy
in a village called Tadem,

who used to decorate
the tops of pastry with cut outs
of fantastic figures;
this is for Zarif
who did needlework
passably well
and figures faster than any man.

This is for Zarif
who prayed with two hands
and who wrote to her son
that although she could not watch him
while he was away at school
she knew he would want to be
like the other good men in his family
who did not smoke.

This is for that simple woman
who did not teach her son
to be a revolutionary
but when revolution came, hid a gun for him
in the garden, against bad days.

This is for Zarif whom the Turks beat,
asking the whereabouts of that son;

for Zarif who said over and over again
I do not know,
although she did.

This is for Zarif whose arm was smashed
then made raw then broken to pieces
then cut off while she repeated when she waked
she did not know.

This is for one-armed Zarif
who lived through hell;
who lived to see her grandchildren
in another world,
this is for her
who once held my right hand in her left
and never told me what I must do with mine.

SONGS OF BREAD*

You think I wrote from love.
You think I wrote from ease.
You imagine me singing as I walked
through wheat, praising bread.
You imagine me looking from my window
at my children in the grass, my wife
humming, my dog running, my sun
still warm. But this notebook is
drenched in blood. It is written in blood
in a wagon rolling past yellow,
amber, gold wheat. But in the dark,
in the smell of sweat, urine, vomit.
The song of blue pitchers filled
with sweet milk, the song of silver
fountains welcoming students home,
the song of silo, barn, harvest,
tiller and red soil, all written
in the dark. The Turks allowed it.
What harm in a pen soon to be theirs,
a notebook to be theirs, a coat,
theirs, unless too much blood splattered.
You read and picture me in

a tranquil village, a church, on
the Bosphorus, on a hillside, not
in anguish, not in fury, not wrenching
back the dead, holding the sun still
for a few more hours, making bread
out of words. This notebook you ransomed,
dear friend, postponed, delayed my storm.
You see only its calm.

*Title of a volume of poems by Armenian poet Daniel Varoujan
published after his death, from his prison notebooks, kept while he
was awaiting his execution (by stoning) at the outset of the Turkish
massacres of the Armenians in 1915. The notebook, Songs of Bread,
containing sunny, pastoral poetry, was sold by his Jailers to an
Armenian priest. The title poem was missing.

TRANSLATING

I would run, run
to escape your blood
filled poems which
my father would recite.
I would dodge the ash
and smoke that hid
in your songs, Siamanto.

And who will bring, who will bring
one handful of that sacred ash
to bury with my exiled bones?

I ran
from tattooed skin that
bore the blue cross, ran
from numbers on the wrists.

I did not want to know
the poetry of wrongs.

And when my father died
and strangers came to say
your lines, a stranger
sprinkled sacred ash,
men who had heard the words
I would not hear.

And now I take your poems
and pound, pound them
into a raw new language
using all the force
of unshed tears.

THREE POETS, 1915

Varoujan

The great Armenian epic,
that is what I was working on.
And when I would read segments
to my students their eyes would fill
with the deep secret of their past.
It was like owning a huge gem
we alone knew about. I polished it
in a secret room. When the Turks
hauled me out in April to my death
they found the stone, still rough,
and tossed it into the great fire.

Siamanto

My greatest rhythms rolled out
when I spoke, resurrecting my people's
hopes. I told them to build muscle
and break the ropes. And when I wrote
I heard Narek breathe in my poems.
Narek set the pace. For centuries
our legacy. Yet so many children do not
claim their inheritance, forbidden to learn
their letters. Some wear his poems
like talismans waiting to learn. I praise
the words that link us stronger than blood.

Tekeyan

Older than one, the same age as the other,
I outlived both only because
I was in Jerusalem when the great crime came.
Brothers, I write every day now,
honing, honing, I rewrite and reshape.

Poems have become my wife and children.
Editorials are my letters home
but to no address that I own. I write out
the burden of having lived,
the terrible burden of having survived.

MISCARRIAGE

The names they picked for you
became more and more
impossible to pronounce
in English. Urartu!
your father shouted
for a boy. Nayirie
for a girl, your mother agreed.
Geography's Arax, Shiraz
edged out the hero's,
Trasdamat, the old king
whose name was kept alive
as General Tro's.
Half jests reviving
everything Armenia
lost, myths, pagan gods
Christian martyrs:
Varoujan, Varak, Vrej,
either sex appropriate
for a fish swimming
three months.
The heavy names piled up
until you came
in a rush of blood
unnamed, losing once again
the old places.

*Urartu and Nayirie are ancient names for Armenia.
Arax is a river.
Shiraz is a place and a poet.

POSTCARD FROM DANIEL VAROUJAN

"In those days," Daniel Varoujan's
daughter Veronica writes,
"they did not take cameras
when they traveled
but brought back photo cards.
Here is one my father brought
from Versailles. I thought you
might like to have it, since
it bears your name."

I hold a postcard
Daniel Varoujan has held,
Diana of Versailles,
a profile, looking like
me if I still looked like me.

He chose this card and said
my name, perhaps,
pronouncing it Deeanna
(as some Armenians do
when commenting on translations
as if Varoujan were theirs).

I think of him as mine
as much, yes, as
his daughter's.

Once she told me: "I never knew him.
I was a baby. But I remember
someone tall and warm, saying
good-bye. Someone who never came
again. He grew even taller.
as grown ups talked. But then
I grew, grew older
than he was that April.
Now I think of him
as my child, a young man

robbed, the way I was robbed
of him."

He is at a museum shop
picking a postcard
to send home. Seventy-five years later
it arrives to another woman
with the name of his marble huntress
who will hold it and weep
for lost mythologies.

*Armenian poet killed by the Turks with 200 other writers and
community leaders in 1915 at the onset of the genocide.

TWO VOICES

"Do you think of yourself as an Armenian? Or an American?
Or hyphenated American?"
                                        —D.M. Thomas

In what language do I pray?

Do I meditate in language?

In what language am I trying
to speak when I wake from dreams?

Do I think of myself as an American,
or simply as woman when I wake?

Or do I think of the date and geography
I wake into, as woman?

Do I think of myself in my clothes
getting wet walking in the rain?

Do I think velvet, or do I think skin?

Am I always conscious of genes and
heredity or merely how to cross my legs
at the ankle like a New England lady?

In a storm do I think of lightning
striking? Or white knives dipped
into my great aunt's sisters'
sisters' blood?

Do I think of my grandfather telling
about the election at the time
of Teddy Roosevelt's third party,

and riding with Woodrow Wilson
in a Main Street parade
in Worcester?

Or do I think of my grandmother
at Ellis Island,

or as an orphan in an Armenian village?

Or at a black stove in Worcester
baking blueberry pie for my grandfather
who preferred food he had grown
to like in lonely mill town
cafeterias while he studied
for night school?

Do I think of them as Armenian
or as tellers of the thousand and
one wonderful tales in two languages?

Do I think of myself as hyphenated?

No. Most of the time, even as you,
I forget labels.

Unless you cut me.

Then I look at the blood.
It speaks in Armenian.

WITHOUT YOU* I AM

a lute	without	strings
strings	without	knots
knots	without	pegs
pegs	without	holes
holes	without	ground
ground	without	seed
seed	without	rain
rain	without	skies
skies	without	wind
wind	without	direction
direction	without	home
home	without	hearth
hearth	without	fire
fire	without	fuel
fuel	without	air
air	without	sun
sun	without	light
light	without	dark
dark	without	sound
sound	without	melody
melody	without	words
words	without	heart
heart	without	hope
hope	without	song
song	without	a lute

*The Armenian language

HOW TO BECOME AN ARMENIAN

"To be Armenian is bad luck
and to choose to remain
is a trial and obligation,"
Avedik Issahakian claims.

But William Saroyan answers
in the spirit of fun:
"Being Armenian means merely
saying you are one."

"After all those massacres,"
my grandfather says,
"to be born at all is a miracle;
to remain just stubbornness."

"To be born Armenian," says my father,
"is to inherit a cause and a case;
to remain Armenian means using
pen, plough and sword."

"To be Armenian means hoping,"
Antranig Zaroukian writes,
"when a plane crash is in the news,
no Armenian is aboard."

To be Armenian means choosing
Hittite and Urartuan roots.
To remain Armenian means eating
history's forbidden fruits.

"To be Armenian you love land
held by others," Tavtian insists.
Remaining Armenian means trusting
justice that does not exist.

"To be born Armenian is to be orphaned,"
Shiraz wrote in his poem.
And to remain is believing
mother and father wait for you at home.

FOR MY FATHER

The windshield wipers
sweep, pushing back the snow
to my childhood and you
singing "Annie Laurie" as we go.

Outside, the road has narrowed
to green glass. A storm.
Inside, as long as you are singing
we are safe and warm.

Outside, crystal trees
reflect the headlight shine.
Inside, you sing "Yerevan,
if only I could see you one more time."

SHIFTING THE SUN

When your father dies, say the Irish,
you lose your umbrella against bad weather.
May his sun be your light, say the Armenians.

When your father dies, say the Welsh,
you sink a foot deeper into the earth.
May you inherit his light, say the Armenians.

When your father dies, say the Canadians,
you run out of excuses. May you inherit
his sun, say the Armenians.

When your father dies, say the French,
you become your own father.
May you stand up in his light, say the Armenians.

When your father dies, say the Indians,
he comes back as the thunder.
May you inherit his light, say the Armenians.

When your father dies, say the Russians,
he takes your childhood with him.
May you inherit his light, say the Armenians.

When your father dies, say the English,
you join his club you vowed you wouldn't.
May you inherit his sun, say the Armenians.

When your father dies, say the Armenians,
your sun shifts forever.
And you walk in his light.

EXILES

My father, listening
to the broadcast news,
my mother said,
was exactly the same
as her father,
intent on every word
as if perhaps
he could lose
something added
since the last was heard.
The Monitor,
The New York Times consumed,
every hour on the hour
hushing the room,
they leaned toward news
that never came.

AT MT. AUBURN CEMETERY

"Defense Secretary Weinberger fears acknowledging genocide by Turks will offend them."

My father is lying in a green
field, green, green under a sun
so hot the yellow wheat and pale
straw have turned green in his eyes.
He closes them. He is fifteen.
The green field is in Armenia.
The sun is the Armenian sun
of 1915. He closes his eyes
and seventy years have passed.
I am lying in a green field
in Massachusetts under a sun
so hot it has turned the yellow
weeds green inside my eyes.
I close them tighter and the entire
field turns red. I touch it
with blind fingers. It is not wet
with either blood or tears
like his fields. "Hairig,"
I say, "I am so sorry.
What can I do? How can I talk to you
when this soil that gave you haven
and home with its government
says you never existed.
What can I say, I who therefore
cannot be here to say it?"

LOOKING AT CAMBODIAN NEWS
PHOTOS

My sack of tiny
bones, bird
bones, my baby
with head so large
your thin neck bends,
my flimsy bag of breath,
all my lost cousins
unfed
wearing your pink flesh
like cloth,
my pink rag doll
with head that grows
no hair,
eyes that cannot close,
my unborn past,
heaving your dry tears.

FLYING OVER THE CAUCASUS

"Who can hold a fire in his hand
by thinking of the frosty Caucasus?"
my seat-mate, the poet from Yerevan
quotes King Richard's lines then begins,
the exiled Pushkin's "O Caucasus ..."
as the ice caps, under a daylight
frozen moon, snow caps of the highest
mountains of my dreams, ripple below
as if in a lunar film.

"O Kovkas! O Caucasus!"
I quote back startling
the bearded poet beside me
who expected more Shakespeare.
"Strike Caucasus! Lash out!
The tear-filled eyes of
a ruined Armenia look
to you for hope."

"You know Siamanto
in America?" he asks.

"You recognize Siamanto
in Russia?" I answer.

He reaches for my hand.
"All Armenians know the same poems."
He improvises now, "Our eyes
can smile while we quote tears.
Strike! Pummel. Beat and flail.
Smash the horizon with your
white staves. Tear the skies
with your rage!"

I answer in English this time, "No,
Caucasus, lie still and grow.
Let your ice envelope,

your stone pellets pelt and
your streams grow cold with fury."

He continues, as if
the English were understood, "Strike
fear into the heart of the Czarist
by showing how you remain
the unconquerable profile."

"The czarist is gone," I laugh, then,
"Look. Look. Look. How white,
how endless, how fathomless."

"Measurable only by poems," he says.

And we sailed on, over
the white sheets below
that were not like Pasternak's
rumpled bed of blue ice,
rising over stagnant heat.

Nor were those mountains,
marching with us
as they did with Charents
row after row
like automatic salvos
from machine guns, swelling
from climax to climax leading
Charents to his red dawn.
This time the mountains were
the white crumpled paper
of our poems.

That night, over Finland
eye-level with a golden moon

and nothing below but ink, I wrote
this for the mountains
and the poet left in Moscow.

O Kovkas,
I too have seen your ice glory, and
from a place once upon a time
only the dead
dreamed of looking from.
O mountains, that named my doomed race,
let me praise you with a different tongue
but with the eyes of a traveler
whose sight is the same
as the horseman's* below
the ice line whose heart
and horse flew
while his song reached above
these metal wings.

*Reference to Varoujan's Pegasus, symbol of freedom.

WHITE NIGHTS, BLACK DAYS

In Finland
I was invited to stay
for the white nights
of summer.
"These dark days
shorten, shorten,"
my host promised as
the light snow fell
in October over
the red beeches darkening
their copper leaves.

"You will stay
and read Finnish poetry,
from the Kalevala
to Kivikkaho you like
so much. And you will
make them as American
as you have made
Daniel Varoujan."

I smiled. Varoujan
was Armenian. And he
stayed Armenian
even in English,
in Russian,
in Japanese.

My Finnish host
continued,
"Varoujan became
international,
became ours,
became everyone's,
once translated.
But if he had been
translated badly
you would have trampled
on his grave."

He does not have
a grave.
He does not have
a grave.
He is not buried
but carried in every heart–
"It is the heart
of a nation beating
in its poetry
that beats the same
in every other heart."

My host and I were
walking under the trees
on a gray street
in Tempere.
"Think about it and write
to us saying you will
come back when it is
the time of white nights.
And we will work
without barriers of light.
And we will play without
barriers of dark."

"Yes," I said,
"I will think about
days that have no night.
And nights with
no morning." And I do
the way one thinks of
roads not traveled,
loves not loved,
days not lived,
except as dreams
dreamed by daylight.

HORSES ON THE ROOF

My father in a storm
of pigeons
in San Marco's Square
points up,
"Now look at those
horses well." His words
bring back Browning's
Last Duchess.

"They're yours,"
he says,
"They came with
Tiridates to Italy
in Nero's day
overland, not
to pollute the sea.
Perfect symbols
of our craft.
They blend bronze
with our tales
of fiery steeds.

"On such a beast
Sanasar flew
into the sun.
Just how these four
were planted
on this roof
is a mystery
to all except tourists
with Armenian blood."

We move in for a closer
view of horses
that can be seen
only from far away.

NO ONE TATTOOED MY SKIN

and pulled off my face.
No one ripped my belly.
I was not taken to Istanbul
for either harem
or experimental
hospital. No one made me
servant or slave.

No one had me crawl
like a dog or grovel
for a piece of bread.

My soul did not fold its wings
and wither, choosing
to drown in the Euphrates
rather than bear another day.

But oh, my sisters,
now that 75 years
have passed and
no one has spoken for you,
I spit out the ink of words
you swallowed unsaid.

THE LONGEST KISS IN THE WORLD

Under a purple beech tree arching
into a perfect gazebo, we had spread
a picnic of papers and strawberries.
Only a year before, we had found
this place and sat stiffly apart. Now
you could fall asleep moving a leg
against mine and I did not move, but
leaned to translate the design
your lashes made. Suddenly I understood
the Armenian word nakhshoun, a mix
of embroidered, and pleasingly
flower-like. Blue eyes opened and for
a long time, while the branches thickened
to shut out other Arboretum trees
and sounds of birds, you kissed me.
The kiss between us lengthened, sweetened,
not with passion but with the three hymns
the bells on a nearby church played.
If that kiss tasted of strawberries I did
not think of fruit, only of the vespers
ringing like a pledge to span my life.

INSIDE GREEN EYES, BLACK EYES

Inside my eye
is another eye
looking out
seeing inside
your eye
looking in.

Inside my voice
that speaks with
spongy soft verbs
is another voice
that shouts
Hayasdan! Hayasdan!

Inside my song
is another song
whose words
I never learned.
I sing. I sang.
The song inside
is never done.

*Hayasdan means "Armenia" in Armenian.

IN MY DREAM

I found the bloodied arm on the ground
before me. "You didn't need it," said the voice.
I saw a sea of dismembered limbs tossed,
strewn to the horizon and beyond.
"You didn't really need these bones."
They covered land that stretched, pressed past.
"You didn't need these provinces, did you?
What would you do with all these stones?"
A mountain of broken bodies rose.
"You didn't need Mt. Ararat, did you?"
I tried to speak. No tongue. My breath froze.
"You didn't need that language, did you?"
I woke, washed, and looked in the glass.
Only another American dressed in fine clothes.

SUNSET

They move slowly,
each with a candle
in orderly procession,
these the executed,
led by the least of them,
the carpenter who had joined
only to be with his friend,
a man of no politics but
with a sense of right.
Second is Levon
who would have joined
any revolution. Third,
Bedros, who believed
in sharing as Christ
taught, although
he did not believe
in Christ. Fourth,
Khosrov, who had loved
liberty since struggling
to untie his swaddling clothes.
Fifth, sixth, seventh, and so on,
each with a candle.
We thought they were rays
of the setting sun.

DROWNING

In your absence, I am learning
to swim again at the Temple Street Y,
Wednesdays. Beginners class.

Buoyed by green air
plunge my face in and
bubble out like a fish

from another life. I move
through the past slowly
arm over arm.

"That's good." Carol shouts
from the rim of the pool.
In a minute she will slide

her eight month pregnant body
into the water hiding her round
suit and the swimmer inside.

"This is the best
exercise for us all," she laughs
when I cough up chlorine
from my stinging nose.

"In the spring all pain
will be forgotten." She leads me
along the ledge to the deep end.

"You are going to tread water.
Let go of the wall. Pedal.
Water wants to hold you up."

The slimy edge of the pool
slips from my grip and
I go down into the blue Pacific,

green Atlantic and the black
leech filled pond in West Auburn,
down and up again. "Carol. Carol."

Carol is teaching someone else,
miles away, listening to the heart
inside her heartbeat,

has abandoned me until spring
when I will not remember pain. I shout
your name now. The YW pool echoes

with the sound of warriors screaming
the name from the hills of Sassoun...
Carol is beside me smiling,

saying, "Wonderful. You tread water
as if it were solid."
She leads me to the ledge.

"No!" I spit out, "No. I was drowning.
I was dying." "Next spring," she says,
"You will be our best swimmer."

SECRET OF LIFE

Once during the war
on a bus going to Portsmouth
a navy yard worker
told me the secret of life.

The secret of life, he said,
can never be passed down
one generation to the other.

The secret of life, he said,
is hunger. It makes an open hand.

The secret of life is money.
But only the small coins.

The secret of life, he said,
is love. You become what you lose.

The secret of life, he said,
is water. The world will end
in flood.

The secret of life, he said,
is circumstance.

If you catch the right bus
at the right time
you will sit next
to the secret teller

who will whisper it
in your ear.

LISTENING TO YOU TALK TO
SOMEONE ELSE

I hear the sound of water,
waves going back to sea.
The fall of unpicked grapes.

Listening to you talk to someone else
I see the long black cedar shadows
of tall women
I have never met.

In the glass you hold,
a new landscape stretches
like a vision of the future
bright as the state of grace
but without one single
recognizable face.

THE RIDDLE

He asked, What flower blooms in winter?
And he asked, What snow falls in summer?
And, What paper is never erased by erasing?

Once in old Armenia there was
(or perhaps there never was*) a custom
for choosing a bride.

Whether the girl were pretty
was not so important
as whether the girl had pretty ways.
And that was not so important
as whether she had people
who smiled the way your people smiled.

But that was not so important as the answers
she could give the riddles.

And she answered,
Snow is the flower that blooms in winter.

And she answered,
Death is the snow that falls in summer.

And she answered,
Memory is the paper that cannot be erased
by erasing.

And the riddles were solved. Or they were not,
depending upon how pretty she was, after all.

*Armenian fairytales begin "Once there was, or perhaps there never was."

MIXED MARRIAGE

He marries the lilac from the Taurus Mountains.
He marries the Cilician Church.
He marries the snows of the Caucasus,
and the Cossacks who will drive
across his dreams. He marries waking
to the sound of the thousand bells of Ani.

He marries the blood sea.
He marries the heart with two million scars
to whom he owes a healing.
He marries unretribution.
He marries village music
and red scarves flying.
He marries pagan dances
and Christian quiet.
He marries the step-child of Russia.

She marries the Mississippi
and Mark Twain,
and the pioneers pushing across the plains.
She marries recipes from Wales.
She marries the blue-eyed West.
She marries Europe's errant son,

the prodigal who made good.

He marries the ashes of Smyrna,
and the dried bones of Dersim.
He marries spring in Kharpert,
the autumn caiques on the Bosphorus.
He marries the Gregorian chant,
a thousand smiling relatives.
He marries a house with an open door.
He marries the knowledge of the fragility,
of life. He marries an Armenian.

She marries the red soil of Texas,
and generosity and the blue Navajo Turquoise.
She marries Lockheed Aircraft,
Wall Street and the Sunday Times,
Seventh Avenue and East
Main Street and the St. Louis Blues.
She marries the Cleveland Museum,
the Boston Symphony
and popcorn.
She marries Harvard, shrimp boats
in Louisiana and California raisins.
She marries the Great Lakes, psychoanalysis,
the PTA and the great white shopping center,
U.S.A.

COUPLES

Sunday afternoons along
the lake, Noah's twos
are strewn everywhere.
I stare at pulley-
ed swans who mate
for life and walking couples
leaning into inverted V's.

Last night I dreamed again
of one-winged birds who
had to fly in pairs.
I was an ancient pihi
too. But the only one I cared
to fly with was left-
winged just like me.

HIS FIRST WIFE

I see her
in the ice palace,
the princess of the north,
fastening her white fox choker.
She steps out into a black
and silver courtyard;
sits on a carved glass
bench to lace on her skates
then glides across
her own summer face
held in the frozen lake.

DAUGHTER

I was the child who swallowed whole
the sight of showmen eating fire,
flying rabbits on piano wire,
every happy ending told,
sure that straw could spin to gold.

I grew older. Gold spun back to straw.
I learned miracles could lie
only in the beholder's eye.
Stayed jaded until the day I saw
two eyes fill with my old awe.

POULTRY

"I thought you were a bird of paradise,
but you're just a silly goose."
                                            —G.B. Shaw

He set out snares,
his own heart as bait
for claws to tear,
his eager flesh in wait
for tropic air
of birds of paradise,
for proud arching neck,
for beaks, for hooded eyes.
What is this peck,
peck, peck?

FORGETTING

After the last pulse
and the first sealing
of my ears I forgot pain.
But not your voice.

I forgot light. It drained
from the edges of the trees
until all shapes blurred.
But not your eyes.

With the folding of my hands
on my breast, I forgot
the unfolding of time.

Then all color
faded past imagining.

With the first thousand years,
or was it the first day,
I forgot the clap of tides
and the touch of water.

With the first shovel
of earth over me I forgot
the sky that held the moon.
But not your eyes.

When my cheek lost
its contour I forgot
the story that was
born into my bones.

Duty and memory, released
them, let them become
one with the other stones.
Then I forgot you.

With the first greening
of earth above me
something like memory stirs.

FISHERMAN'S MOTHER

She scours fish,
steel fish, lead fish,
once still, once spume,
once ray.
And thinks of him
once voice, once flesh,
now rain, now foam,
now spray.

GAME

Artemis paints her face today
in a faint blush disguise,
outlining eyes, accentuates
a sweet but sham surprise.
And to anticipate the taste
of prey, her lips are glazed
with scarlet berry overlays.
Then she lacquers, then she sprays
musk on her throat and throws
on her wolfskin coat and goes
out to disobey the law of meat
that lets one hunt enough to eat
and only that. That's not her aim.
The hunt itself is bigger game.

FROM A NERJA HOTEL WINDOW

(For Helen Pahigian)

The voices of the women of Spain
are like the wines of Malaga
made from long white grapes,
sweet but not sweeter
than the green sunshine
of early morning.

The voices of the women of Spain
are low but filled
with tense threads of laughter,
the sound of two sisters
talking after long separation.

UNNATURAL RHYTHMS

1
Poetry, says the teacher,
comes in natural rhythms,
unless it is interrupted
by unnatural silence.
Poetry, says the teacher,
began with the beat of the heart
the iamb of the march
left, right, left, RIGHT.
It slaps in and out
like the breath
of the ocean
unless it is interrupted
by unnatural silence.
Poetry, says the teacher,
ebbs with the moon,
but unnatural rhythms
can shake you awake
especially the unnatural
silence of poets in 1915.

2
Don't ride a train,
the obstetrician advises.
The rhythm is the same
as birth and induces labor pains.

Everything is replaced by
science and technology
except rhythm and old songs.

The clattering wheels are
replaced by high speed rails.
Whirring planes and helicopters create
the metaphors for change.
Helicopters, bicycles and trains.

3
Was it a movie, a dream
a scene from another life,
you in khaki,
me in white,
the train unclasping
our clasped hands
and pulling us apart?

The old films
on night-time TV,
the honeymoon train
with rhythms of the wheels,
rhythms of rains,
the soldier in the train
window waving good-bye good-bye

brings you back waving
Diana, wait

as I pass on the hot street,
my warped bike wheeling
a new rhythm.

You run toward me asking
What happened!

My arm is dripping blood.
You lead me into the gasoline
station where you are working
for the summer.

You wash my arm. I let you
because it will spare my mother's
fright when I walk in.

You tell me I need a doctor for
stitches: "Your heart
is overworked trying to heal this."
Should you close the station
and come with me?

I laugh and tell you I'm fine.
I have walked miles
since I fell
at the bottom of a country hill
and have been passed by classmates
who waved, seeing only an unwounded side.

My arm stops hurting
and I look at you for the first time.

Someone two classes ahead of me
who plays football in another world,
not mine. Now you know what war is like,
you joke.
No. Not yet.

Two weeks later you were gone.
Two months later, letters from Southeast Asia.

I never think of you
except when old movies
are rerun or I tend a cut
and wonder who washed the blood.

TRANSLATING

I am sitting in a cafe in Prague
in my 1960 dancer's body
next to the table
where Marina Tsvetayeva,
tears in her eyes, waits
for you, anticipating
the kiss you will give.

She lights her cigarette
and looks up at you, hurrying
toward her, impatient
for the sweetness
to be transferred from
her tongue to yours.

I tense against the sight
of you rushing toward her.
You see only the blue lake
of her eyes where illusions
ride out the storm.

And I on the edge of despair
taste as much joy as you
on the brink of a poem
making much of time.

OPEN POEM

death lies beside each sleeper
that day wakes up
stalks every step
puts down the heel
that pace picks up again
and exhales every breath
except where love breathes in

WHAT THE DEAD DON'T KNOW

The dead know the difference
between half and whole.
They know what is laughable.
And the biggest joke of all.

They've learned how to sleep,
to ignore flux and flow.
They know what to keep,
and what to let go.

The dead know what to love.
It is settled now.
They know what to smile at.
But have forgotten how.

ON BEING ASKED TO SUPPLY DATE
AND PLACE OF BIRTH

I am thirteen years old.
Forever. Pasternak said
he was fourteen. But I am
younger. Just starting
but no longer a child. And
aging fast. Although
the world stays new and
wet behind the ears. I just begin
to understand that I will never
understand. And I am in love
as if for the first time with
the written word. This affair
began when my grandfather promised
me that true love would always be
returned. I was conceived in 1915
when the blood of my other grandparents
soaked through the earth of Kharpert
and seeped, seeped until the thirties
when it reached Worcester, Massachusetts.
I was born in a garden when war cracked
the face of the earth that had not listened
to the 1915 blood. I was born in the New
York City subway when everyone turned
to stare at my American legs.
I was born in the Boston University
Mugar Library the first time
I heard Gerard Manley Hopkins
playing with words. I arrived
after difficult labor in the seventies
attended by physicians named Narek,
Siamanto and Varoujan who decided I might be
worth saving. That was thirteen years ago.

FOR THE UNSAID

Letterless, tongueless, and unpronounced
the words sleep under their own heaviness.
Do not disturb them.

Their silence is not golden,
is not assent, is not guilty.
Their silence is not the handmaiden
of death. They will wake
in their own time.

They are in that silent place,
the eye of the storm,
the edge of the heart,

the day before it knows
it is struck down. Let the words
wake themselves.

BIOGRAPHICAL NOTE

Diana Der-Hovanessian, New England-born poet, is the author of thirteen books of poetry and translations, and has won international and national awards and fellowships, including prizes from the Poetry Society of America, the Columbia/P.E.N. Translation Center, and the Massachusetts Arts Council. She is president of the New England Poetry Club and works as a visiting poet and guest lecturer on American poetry, translation, and the literature of human rights at various universities. In 1993-94 she was an NEA and a Fulbright Fellow.

PUBLICATIONS BY DIANA DER-HOVANESSIAN

How to Choose Your Past, Ararat Press, Saddle Brook,
   New Jersey
About Time, Ashod Press, New York
Inside Green Eyes, Black Eyes, translated into Armenian,
   Sovetpress, Yerevan, Armenia
Songs of Bread, Songs of Salt, Ashod Press, New York
Selected Poems, Sheep Meadow Press, New York

TRANSLATIONS

Anthology of Armenian Poetry, Columbia University Press,
   New York (winner of P.E.N./Translation Center and
   Kolligian Awards)
Land of Fire, Selected Poems of Eghishe Charents, Ardis
   Press, Ann Arbor, Michigan (winner of Van de
   Bovenkamp, Armand Erpf Awards for excellence in
   literary translation)
Sacred Wrath, Selected Poems of Vahan Tekeyan, Ashod
   Press, New York
The Arc, Selected Poems of Shen-Mah, St. Vartan Press,
   New York (The above four edited with M. Margossian)
Come Sit Beside Me and Listen to Kouchag (Medieval
   Armenian poems) Ashod Press, New York
Selected Poems of Gevorg Emin, International Poetry Forum
   Press, Pittsburgh (limited edition)
For You on New Year's Day, Selected Poems of Gevorg Emin,
   Ohio University Press, Athens, Ohio
Coming to Terms, Selected Poems of Vahan Derian, Ashod
   Press, New York